HAL LEONARD BARITONE GUITAR METHOD

BY CHAD JOHNSON

T0079474

Speed • Pitch • Balance • Loop

To access audio, visit:
www.halleonard.com/mylibrary

Enter Code
4064-4372-6196-7441

ISBN 978-1-5400-0038-5

Visit Hal Leonard Online at
www.halleonard.com

Contact Us:
Hal Leonard
7777 West Bluemound Road
Milwaukee, WI 53213
Email: info@halleonard.com

In Europe contact:
Hal Leonard Europe Limited
42 Wigmore Street
Marylebone, London, W1U 2RN
Email: info@halleonardeurope.com

In Australia contact:
Hal Leonard Australia Pty. Ltd.
4 Lentara Court
Cheltenham, Victoria, 3192 Australia
Email: info@halleonard.com.au

CONTENTS

INTRODUCTION

Welcome to the *Hal Leonard Baritone Guitar Method*. In this book, we'll examine the baritone guitar and what makes it so unique in the world of fretted instruments. We'll talk about its famous purveyors and some of the confusion that surrounds it with regard to tuning, scale, and string gauges. But most importantly, we'll focus on what it does well and why, and we'll use music examples and real-world songs to learn how to recreate those sounds.

If you already own a baritone, then feel free to get crackin'! If not, then definitely take a look at the Gear Talk section to help you make the most informed purchase possible. Not all baritones are made the same, and it's important that you choose the one that'll do what you want it to do. Do you want an electric or an acoustic? What style of music are you going to play with it? Does it need a vibrato bar? All of these questions are important to ask up front.

The baritone can provide an entirely new arsenal of sounds in the studio and "wow" live audiences with its charm. It can unlock doors to creativity and inject new life into seemingly tired musical ideas. And it can stamp an indelible sonic mark onto a song with its unique voice. But most of all, it's a joy to play, so enjoy the journey!

HISTORY OF THE BARITONE

The baritone guitar is a bit of a mysterious beast with somewhat of a shrouded history. Although it's difficult to pinpoint exactly when the acoustic baritone guitar (or variations of it) first surfaced—opinions range from 100 years ago to as far back as the 15th century—it's mostly agreed upon that Danelectro released the first electric baritone guitar in 1956. Although not terribly popular at the time, it did find a niche in Nashville. Country artists would use it to add "tic-tac" bass lines to their recordings—essentially doubling the bass guitar for a thicker texture. Other manufacturers soon began to create similar instruments, including Fender's Fender VI in 1961. This was a six-string instrument that was tuned exactly one octave lower than a standard guitar. In other words, its lowest four strings are the same pitch as a bass guitar. The tone is slightly different, however, due to the shorter scale length.

And this brings us to our next bit of debate: what exactly *is* a baritone guitar? Some people consider the Fender VI (later known as the Fender Bass VI) to be a baritone guitar, while others do not. Many consider a baritone guitar to be an instrument that sits between the range of a guitar and a bass (we'll talk about specific tunings in a bit), and that's basically the view we'll take with this book. Over the past few decades, that seems to be where most manufacturers fall within the spectrum, and although there is still plenty of wiggle room with regard to what can be considered "standard" for a baritone, the idea that it sits sonically between a guitar and a bass has been largely embraced by the majority of players and builders.

One of the best-known early endorsers of the baritone guitar was undoubtedly Duane Eddy, who began employing it as early as 1959 on songs like "Bonnie Came Back" and "Kommotion." In fact, he made almost exclusive use of his Danelectro baritone on his *The Twang's the Thang* album (1959). Eddy did not, however, use a baritone on the "Peter Gunn" theme, which is a common misconception. By 1960, the instrument also began showing up in spaghetti western films, so named because they were mostly produced and directed by Italians, and many were shot in Italy. The tic-tac bass was a common application in this genre, as well.

As evidenced with the "Peter Gunn" theme, however, many people often mistake standard guitars for baritones just because they're playing a low-register melody with a twangy tone. This will not do! In this book, we'll celebrate the uniqueness of this instrument and examine the qualities that make it so thoroughly enjoyable and applicable to many styles. So, without further ado, let's get *down* to business.

TYPES OF BARITONES

If you bought this book before purchasing a baritone guitar, be sure to read this section before heading to the music store. Though they're still dwarfed by the number of standard guitars and basses on the market, there are a fair number of baritones available these days. If you know what you're looking for, you'll make a more informed purchase.

Scale Lengths and String Gauges

The *scale length* on a stringed instrument is the distance between the bridge and the nut. A standard electric guitar normally has a scale range of 25.5 inches (Fender style) or 24.75 inches (Gibson style), while an electric bass guitar generally has a scale length of 34 inches. As you may suspect, a baritone guitar will usually have a scale length in between the two.

Scale length affects several factors, including playability, tone, and tuning. Players with small hands generally prefer instruments with smaller scale lengths. The difference between a Fender and a Gibson, 0.75 of an inch, may not seem like a lot, but anyone experienced with both will tell you that it's quite noticeable. Therefore, it's certainly something to consider with the baritone guitar, which has an even larger scale length. It's definitely recommended to get your hands on an instrument to try out before buying, if at all possible.

Most baritone guitars have a scale length of 29.75 inches, but 30 inches is also common, especially on models by Fender. The longer the scale length, the lower the pitch of the strings can be while still retaining a usable tension. In other words, you could tune your standard guitar down a 4th (E to B), but the strings will be pretty floppy at that point. If you use larger gauge strings in order to compensate, it increases the tension on the neck. This is why it's no surprise that baritone guitars, which have a range that falls in between a standard guitar and a bass, typically have a scale length that falls between a standard guitar and bass.

With regard to string gauges, you'll typically find an electric baritone strung with 0.014 to 0.068, which are described as a medium set. A light set will usually span from 0.013 to 0.062. However, some sets, such as Ernie Ball's 6 String Baritone Slinky, span from 0.013 to 0.072, which would work better for lower tunings. A medium acoustic baritone set typically spans from 0.016 to 0.070. It's recommended that you try out some different sets during your first few months with the instrument to see what feels and sounds best. At around $10 a set, it's a worthwhile investment considering the amount of time you'll spend playing it!

Ernie Ball 2839 6 String Baritone Slinky Strings

D'Addario EXL157 Medium Baritone Strings

Electric Baritones

Electric baritones are more common than acoustic, and that's going to be most of the focus in this book. Although electric baritones have a place in many styles, there seem to be three that are most common: '60s-style surf/spaghetti western, country, and metal. Let's examine a few desired characteristics for each.

One of the most obvious differences between the genres will be the type of pickups used. Single-coil pickups such as those found on Fender, Squier, and Danelectro models are generally preferred for the surf/spaghetti western sound. The latter was the weapon of choice for Duane Eddy, and you can find the reissued Danelectro '56 Baritone for a little over $400 new. It's tuned from B (string 6) to B (string 1) and features two "lipstick" single-coil pickups and a 29.75-inch scale length. Squier currently makes the Vintage Modified Baritone Jazzmaster, which is tuned A to A and features a 30-inch scale length, basswood body, maple neck, rosewood fretboard, and a price tag of $450 new. If you're in need of a vibrato-bar system but would still like a vintage-styled sound, you can check out the Gretsch G5265 ($550 new). It features a Bigsby vibrato tailpiece, mini-humbuckers, alder body, maple neck, rosewood fretboard, and a 29.75-inch scale length. Any of these options would do fine in the country genre, as well.

Danelectro '56 Baritone   Gretsch G5265 Baritone

For metal and rock applications, you'll most likely want to get a baritone equipped with humbuckers. Hagstrom makes the Viking Baritone, which sports a semi-hollow design, and therefore would provide a bit of versatility if you wanted to venture into jazzier or bluesier realms, as well. It features a flamed maple body, maple neck, bridge humbucker and neck P-90 (each with their own volume and tone knobs), a standard three-way selector switch, and a price tag of $680 new. For more of a no-frills approach, you can check out the ESP LTD Viper-200B. For $350, you get two humbuckers, a master volume knob, a master tone knob, a basswood body, and a maple neck with rosewood fretboard. For a truly versatile instrument, you can check out the PRS SE 277—the guitar featured on the cover of this book. It features a mahogany body with a gorgeous maple top, a set-in maple neck, two humbucking pickups, and a three-way pickup selector switch. It ships with a gig bag and has a price tag of $750.

ESP LTD Viper-200B   PRS SE 277

It should be mentioned that the three models mentioned above feature shorter scale lengths than the Danelectro, Squier, and Gretsch guitars. The ESP LTD Viper-200B measures at 27 inches, the PRS at 27.75 inches, and the Hagstrom at 28 inches. The PRS SE 277 ships with B-to-B tuning, but the Hagstrom Viking and ESP LTD Viper-200B don't specify the shipped tuning. A B-to-B tuning would certainly work well on either guitar, but A to A may start to get a bit floppy on the Viper-200B.

Needless to say, the difference between 27 inches (Viper-200B) and 30 inches (Squier Vintage Modified Baritone Jazzmaster) is quite noticeable, and if hand size is a concern, that may be the deciding factor for you. Again, this will also depend on what you plan on using the guitar for. This is why it's important to get one in your hands to try out first, as this is the only real way you can determine what feels best. After all, scale length is not the only thing that matters in this regard. It could also be that a volume knob is placed in a spot that conflicts with your picking technique, or the bridge sits at a strange spot for you, etc. Things like this can only be determined with the guitar in hand.

Acoustic Baritones

On the unplugged side of things, the options are a bit skimpier—at least in the more affordable range. Alvarez makes the Artist series ABT60 and ABT60E, the latter including a B-Band SYS550 pickup system. The guitars feature a solid Sitka spruce top, mahogany back and sides, mahogany neck, and rosewood fretboard. With a 27.75-inch scale length, both models ship tuned B to B and can be had for $400 and $500, respectively. The Ibanez AELBT1 features similar specs— spruce top, mahogany back and sides, and mahogany neck—but also includes a cutaway. A Fishman Sonicore pickup and Ibanez AEQ-SP2 preamp round out the features, the scale length is 27 inches, and it goes for $400. Beyond that, you're looking at spending over $1,000 for options by Martin, Taylor, or custom builders.

Alvarez ABT60   Ibanez AELBT1

Martin MSP7700 Lifespan Phosphor Bronze Baritone Acoustic Guitar Strings

A NOTE ON TUNINGS

As mentioned previously, there is not a single standard tuning for baritone guitar. In fact, there's not even one standard definition of what a baritone guitar is, as some people consider the Fender Bass VI a baritone, for example, while others do not. To confuse matters more, it became common practice by the late '60s and early '70s for people to start stringing the Bass VI with lighter gauges and tuning it A to A or B to B, as is the case with most baritones nowadays. This, no doubt, helped lend credence to the idea that the Bass VI could be considered a baritone.

That said, by today's standards, if there's one tuning that's the closest to a "standard" baritone tuning, it's the B-to-B tuning (i.e., a perfect 4th lower than a standard guitar). Most of the guitars listed in the previous section will ship in this tuning, and it's the most widely used baritone tuning overall. Therefore, in this book, we'll be using this tuning throughout: B–E–A–D–F#–B (low to high).

NOTATION CONVENTIONS USED IN THIS BOOK

Since the baritone guitar falls between the range of the standard guitar and the bass, the question of notation arises. How should it be treated? When a standard guitar is tuned down a half step to E♭, it's still notated in standard pitch (i.e., the open sixth string is still called an E) and a footnote simply specifies that the song sounds a half step lower than written. In fact, this is usually the case for any tuning in which all strings are tuned down by the same amount (down a whole step, down 1-1/2 steps, etc.).

But the baritone sounds a full perfect 4th (2-1/2 steps) lower than a standard guitar. In other words, when you play the open sixth string on a baritone, it sounds a B instead of an E. So, the question is: should you write music for the baritone at sounding pitch, or should you continue the process of notating it at standard guitar pitch and simply add a footnote to specify the fact that it's sounding at a lower pitch?

Well, because most baritone guitar players didn't start on a baritone—they most likely started on a standard guitar—we're going to use a bit of a hybrid approach. First of all, we won't be using standard notation in this book (with the exception of a vocal staff on a few songs); we'll instead be using a system called *rhythm tab*. This is basically a system that combines standard tab with rhythmic symbols (stems, ties, dots, etc.) to convey both pitch and rhythm. If this is new to you, check out the legend in the back of the book for a more thorough explanation.

Additionally, we'll be accounting for both the sounding pitch and the guitar-based fingering throughout the book. In other words, if you finger a standard open E chord on a baritone guitar, it will sound a B major chord. So, we're going to show both of these. The sounding pitch chord symbol will be on top, and the guitar-based symbol will be below it in parentheses.

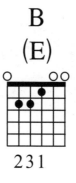

In a way, we'll be treating the baritone guitar as a transposing instrument, not unlike a trumpet. A typical B♭ trumpet reads a C on the page but sounds a B♭ note. A baritone guitar reads what's usually an E note but sounds a B. (In fact, a standard guitar is technically a transposing instrument, too; it's just that it sounds one octave lower than written. So, an E is still an E, etc.) This way, it will be clear how your standard guitar riffs can be adopted to baritone, but you'll also be learning their sounding pitch, as well. Be sure to check out the Additional Things to Keep in Mind section, which will aid you in the process of "thinking fast" when you're jamming with other instruments and need to play in their key.

GEAR TALK

We've looked at several choices in the way of baritone guitars, but an electric baritone doesn't do much damage on its own, of course; it needs an amp to rattle the walls. So, let's take a look at some tried-and-true options that will help you nail the tones you desire.

SURF/SPAGHETTI WESTERN

Amplifier

Since these styles lived mostly in the '60s, it only makes sense that you'll want an amp that's designed to mimic amps of those days. Although many vintage amps can command a pretty penny on the used market, fortunately for us, there are many reissues of classic amps—not to mention newer models based on classic designs—that will fit the bill nicely.

First off, you'll want a tube amp, as they'll break up ever so slightly in the musical way so prevalent in those early recordings. A Fender Deluxe Reverb or its higher-watted cousin, the Fender Twin Reverb, would be prime choices in this regard. Both are available as reissues and can be found used for around $550 and $650, respectively. A Peavey Classic 30, which can be found for $300 used, would also do the trick. Both Fender amps include reverb and tremolo (although it's labeled as "vibrato" on the Fender amps), both of which are essential for the style. The Peavey contains reverb but no tremolo.

But don't count out vintage amps just yet! There are many bargains that can be found, such as a Gibson Skylark GA-5T (around $300), Ampeg Reverberocket or Reverberocket II (around $400), or a Silvertone 1484 piggyback amp/cabinet (about $450). All of these have reverb and tremolo as well, save for the Skylark GA-5T, which has tremolo but no reverb. However, you could easily pair it with a reverb pedal (see Effects section) and be good to go.

Fender Deluxe Reverb

Peavey Classic 30

Effects

The main effects you'll want for this style are reverb (preferably spring reverb) and tremolo (again, this is mislabeled as "vibrato" on Fender amps). An analog or tape-style delay pedal could also serve you well at times. The good news is that many amps will come with spring reverb. If they don't, however, you have several options, including the TC Electronic Hall of Fame ($150 new), Boss FRV-1 '63 Fender Reverb ($100 new), and Behringer RV600 Reverb Machine ($50 new), to name a few. The main thing you'll want to make sure of is that the pedal is able to emulate the spring reverb sound.

Tremolo pedals are widely available. Check out the Electro-Harmonix XO Stereo Pulsar ($90 new), Boss TR-2 Tremolo ($100 new), or the Carl Martin Surf Trem ($86 new) for great-sounding affordable options. For a delay pedal, you'll want one that emulates a tape or analog delay, such as an MXR M169 Carbon Copy ($135 new), Rogue Analog Delay ($50 new), or a Keeley Magnetic Echo Delay ($125 new).

Boss FRV-1 '63 Fender Reverb

Electro-Harmonix XO Stereo Pulsar

COUNTRY

Amplifier

For country tone, you'll generally want an amp that can stay pretty clean for the most part; the Fender Twin would be a great start, but the Peavey Classic 30 will do nicely, as well (you just won't be able to get as loud before it breaks up). Another nice option is the Vox AC30C2, which you can snag for around $550 used. Its little brother, the Vox AC15C1, is another great-sounding amp, albeit with less clean headroom.

Fender Vintage Reissue '65 Twin Reverb

Vox AC30C2

Effects

You'll want to have reverb for sure, and all of the previously mentioned amps do have it. But if you go with an option that doesn't, you can refer to the reverb pedal suggestions for the surf/spaghetti western style. Another must-have in the country world is a compressor pedal. A few tried-and-true models include the Boss CS-3 ($100 new), MXR M-102 Dyna Comp ($80 new), and the Keeley 4-Knob ($200 new). This will help you get the snappy tone that's so common in the genre. You'll probably also want to have a delay pedal, especially for the slapback sound, and all of the options listed in the surf/spaghetti western section would do just fine in this regard.

Boss CS-3 Compression Sustainer

MXR M-102 Dyna Comp

HARD ROCK/METAL

Amplifier

For heavier styles, you'll generally want a "master volume" type tube amp with at least two channels (clean and distorted) and adjustable preamp gain, which basically means it will usually have a knob labeled "distortion" or "gain." This will allow you to get very distorted tones at volumes that won't peel the paint off the walls. A very popular choice is a Mesa/Boogie "rectifier" type amp, such as the Dual Rectifier. Boogies are quite pricey, however, and a Dual Rectifier head alone will run you about $800 used, if you're lucky. This means you'll still need a speaker cabinet, which will be several hundred at least, depending on what speaker configuration you go with. There are some combo options from Boogie, as well, such as the Recto-Verb 25, which features one 12-inch speaker and two channels (each with its own reverb setting) and can be found for around $700 used.

Other, more affordable options are the Blackstar HT Club 40, which has 40 watts, one 12-inch speaker, two channels, and digital reverb. You can find them used for $300. For around $400 used, the Peavey 6505+ is a 60-watt combo with one 12-inch speaker, two channels, and spring reverb, and would handle the job nicely.

Mesa/Boogie Recto-Verb 25

Blackstar HT Club 40

Effects

Effects tend to be used liberally in metal and hard rock, and this includes the *types* of effects, as well. Common ones include reverb, wah-wah, delay, chorus, tremolo, harmonizer, and more. For this reason, you'll do well to check out a multi-effects unit, many of which will contain dozens of effects within one pedalboard unit. The Boss ME-80 ($300 new), Line 6 POD HD500X ($400 new), and the Digitech RP1000 ($300 new) are all affordable choices with extreme versatility. The benefit of these devices is that they also include many different amp simulation models in addition to the effects. You can choose to turn the amp simulation feature off when using them in front of an amp, or you can engage the amp simulation to use them as a direct recording solution in a studio. Each one also features an expression pedal, which can be assigned to control various parameters, such as volume or wah, and you can store your own preset patches for instant recall. Most also include bonus features as well, such as an onboard tuner, a looper, and more.

Line 6 POD HD500X

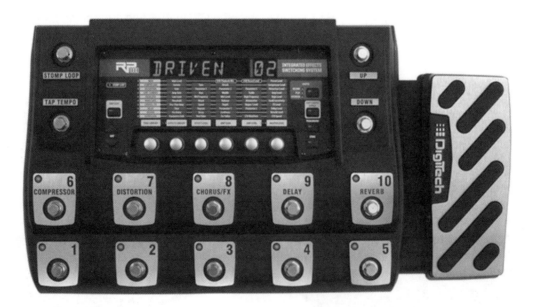

Digitech RP1000

A NOTE ON INTERVALS

You may have heard before that a guitar is tuned "mostly in 4ths" or that a baritone guitar is tuned "a 4th lower than a standard guitar." So, what do we mean by this? Well, let's talk briefly about the subject of intervals, which deals specifically with how the baritone differs from a standard guitar.

An *interval* is the musical distance between notes. In other words, it measures how much higher or lower one note is from another. There are two components of an interval: the *quantity* and the *quality*. For now, we're going to focus on the former.

COUNTING NOTE NAMES

An interval's quantity simply deals with counting. As you may know, the musical alphabet uses seven different letters: A through G. Once you reach either end, you simply start over again.

F – G – A – B – etc.
C – B – A – G – etc.

To measure the interval quantity between two notes, you simply count the letter names involved. So, to measure the interval from a C note up to an E note, for example, you just count through the musical alphabet to see how many note names are involved:

C (1) – D (2) – **E** (3)

So, from C up to E is a 3rd because there are three note names involved: C, D, and E. Let's try a few more.

From A up to E:
A (1) – B (2) – C (3) – D (4) – **E** (5) = a 5th

When measuring the interval between one note and a note below it, you can either choose to count down, or you can simply count up from the lower note. Many people prefer the latter method—always measuring from the lower note—because it keeps the counting consistent.

From G down to F:
Count down from G: **G** (1) – **F** (2) = a 2nd
Or count up from F: **F** (1) – **G** (2) = a 2nd

From A up to B:
A (1) – **B** (2) = a 2nd

From D up to G:
D (1) – E (2) – F (3) – **G** (4) = a 4th

From E down to B (or from B up to E):
B (1) – C (2) – D (3) – **E** (4) = a 4th

And that's all there is to interval quantity. It only deals with note letter names. Sharps and flats don't change anything in this regard. If there are three note names (i.e., letters) involved, it's technically some kind of 3rd. If there are six note names involved, it's some kind of 6th, and so on.

Now that you know that, take a look at that last example above—from E down to B—once more. We said this was a 4th. This is, of course, the difference between a standard guitar's sixth string (E) and a baritone guitar's sixth string (B). The baritone is tuned a *4th lower* than a standard guitar. Now you know what that means!

TO BE SPECIFIC...

If you want to get specific, a baritone is tuned a *perfect* 4th lower than a standard guitar. The "perfect" in this case is the other half of the interval's name: the quality. The *quality* is the part that deals with adding sharps or flats, if necessary. We don't need to get into that right now, but if you'd like to know more about it, there are a number of music theory-related guitar books that will explain it thoroughly. Check out *Guitarist's Guide to Scales Over Chords* or *Music Theory for Guitarists* (both published by Hal Leonard) to learn more.

Regardless, a perfect 4th is the most common type of 4th, and when someone simply says "It's a 4th higher," for example, with no other information, it's a safe bet they're talking about a perfect 4th.

GETTING ACCLIMATED TO OPEN CHORDS

Now that we have the preliminaries out of the way, let's get down to making some music. The first thing you need to know about the baritone guitar is that you can play it just like a normal guitar! It's not like a mandolin or violin, both of which are tuned in 5ths and therefore require you to learn all new chords and scales. All the chord shapes, scales, and riffs you know on a standard guitar will still work on the baritone; they'll just sound a 4th lower.

Of course, the fact that they are a 4th lower isn't insignificant; it may change the way you decide to play your chords. The lower pitch may make some chords sound a bit too muddy with a certain type of tone, or it may be exactly what you're looking for! Just as with any instrument, this is all a matter of personal taste, and it's up to you to decide how you're going to use the instrument.

Let's begin by taking a look at some open chords and hearing how they sound in various progressions and with various tones. As mentioned in the introduction, we'll be naming these chords throughout the book in two ways: the sounding pitch will be indicated by the top chord symbol, and the standard guitar pitch will be indicated by the bottom symbol in parentheses.

Major Chords

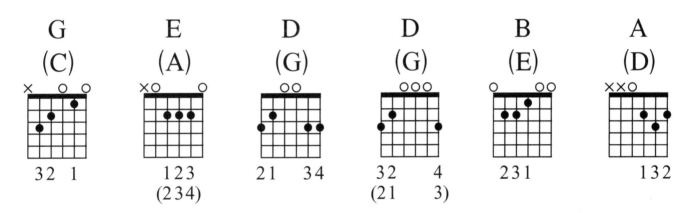

Minor Chords

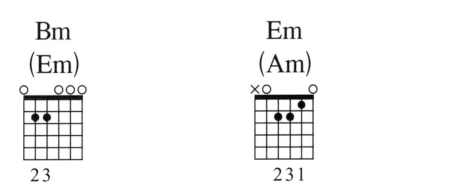

STRUMMING RIFFS WITH OPEN CHORDS

Now let's hear how some of these open chords sound in several strumming riffs. In particular, pay attention to the clarity and power of each chord within the context of each riff. Make a mental (or written) note of which chords you think sound great and which ones (if any) don't sound so hot.

This first example gives you a good representation of what makes the baritone so awesome: those big, thick strings ringing away with some wide-open chords.

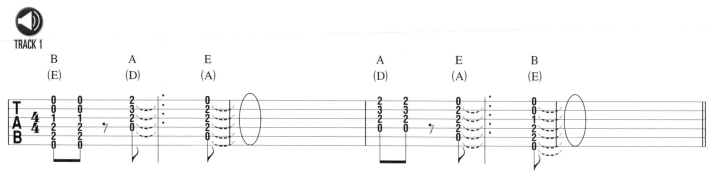

In these next two examples, pay close attention to the G (C) and D (G) chords, both of which have a major 3rd interval on the bottom instead of a perfect 5th, as shown in the other chords.

Major 3rd Interval

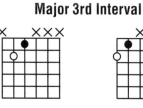

Perfect 5th Interval

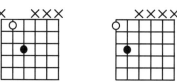

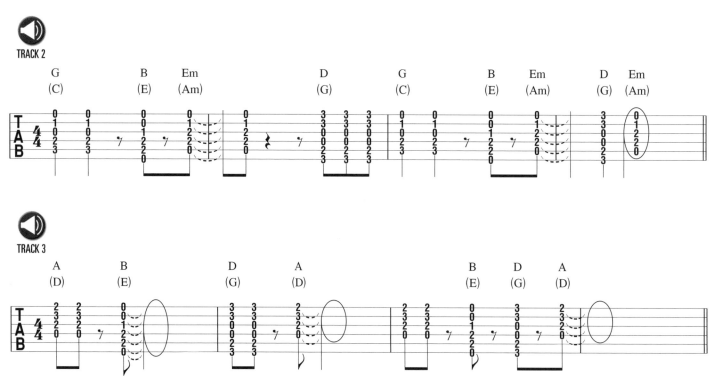

These 3rd intervals can sometimes sound a bit muddy when played this low, depending on the musical context. We'll come back to this idea in a bit and talk about our options for getting around this possible muddiness.

For this next one, we add some palm-muted bass notes before each chord for maximum girth!

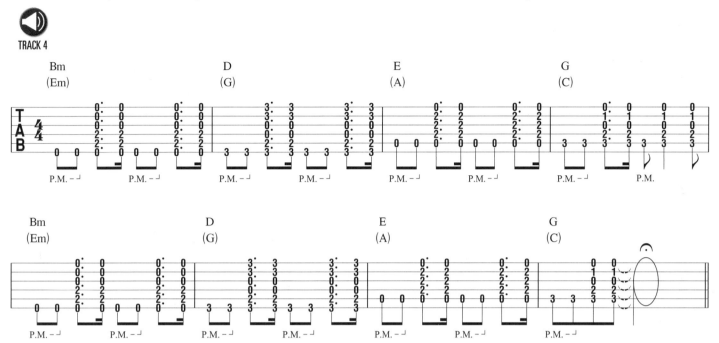

Suspended Chords

Let's add some open suspended chords to our arsenal.

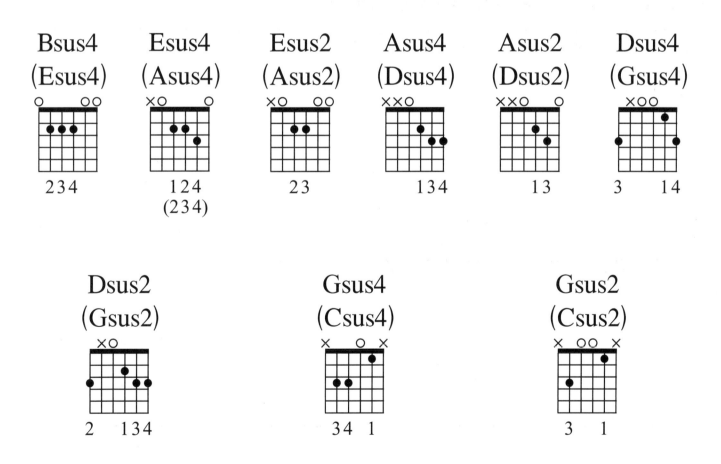

These sus chords can sound huge on the baritone!

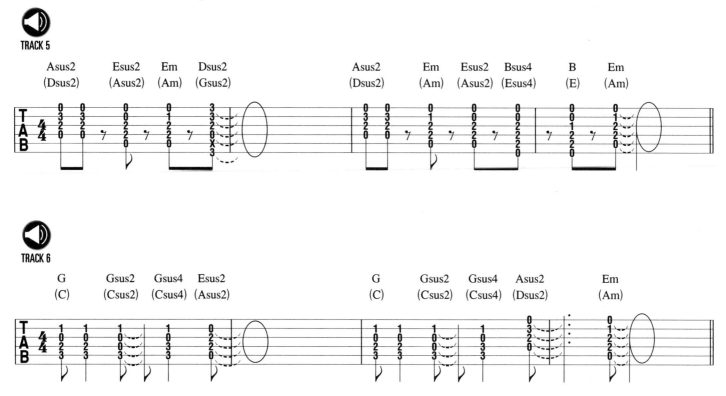

Notice how many of these riffs allow one of the chords to sustain for a bit. This exploits the unique characteristic of the baritone, as these sustained chords have much more sonic weight than their standard guitar counterparts.

ARPEGGIO RIFFS WITH OPEN CHORDS

Now let's try arpeggiating these chords to hear how it sounds on the baritone. This technique can really sound great, as you get a thick yet chiming sound with your arpeggios.

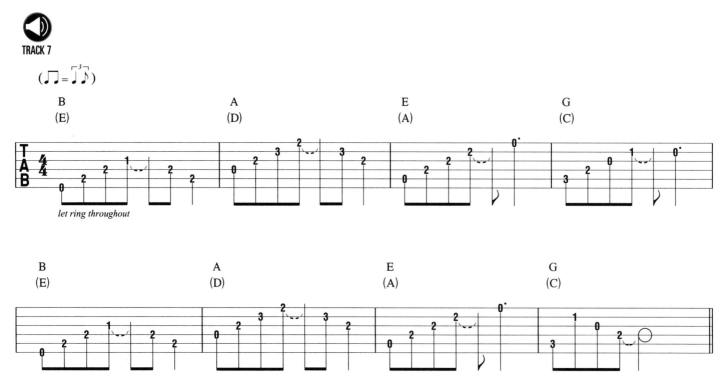

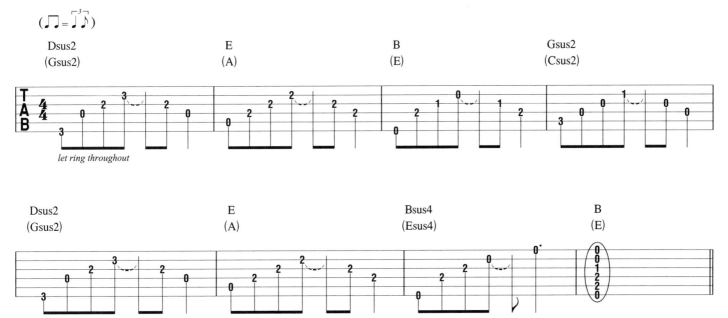

TRACK 9

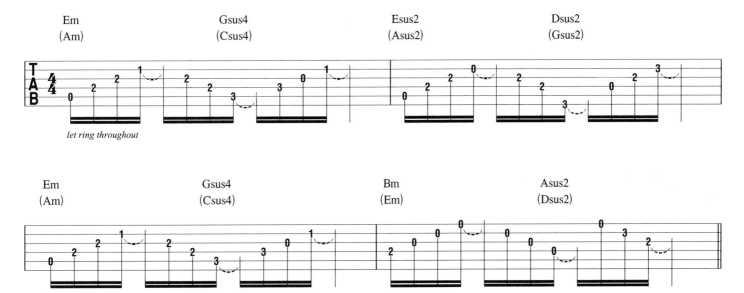

"THE SPACE BETWEEN"

Let's hear how these chords sound in a real-world situation. Dave Matthews played a Jerry Jones SingleCut Baritone on this song, which is a great mixture of the strummed and arpeggiated chords we've looked at thus far. There are two main baritone guitar parts on this song: one for the verses and bridge and one for the choruses. The part shown as Gtr. 2 is simply an arrangement of the synth chords played in the chorus. However, it should be noted that these are essentially the voicings that Dave plays for the chorus when performing this song live, so it's helpful to learn them, as well.

Gtr. 1 Part

Gtr. 1 starts the song by strumming big open E (A) and Dsus2 (Gsus2) chords for the verse, allowing the Dsus2 (Gsus2) to ring for a full measure and a half. The voicings are very near to what we've looked at so far, save for the fact that the top string has been omitted.

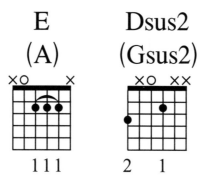

For the bridge, Dave thins out the texture a bit, relying solely on an octave shape on strings 5 and 3 to imply the harmony.

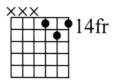

Gtr. 3 Part

Gtr. 3 enters in the chorus with an arpeggio based off the open D shape, only an octave higher. Notice that he's playing an *ostinato* here—a phrase that repeats atop the changing chords. The baritone makes these chiming arpeggios sound huge, and a slight chorus effect is added to thicken the texture even more.

THE SPACE BETWEEN

Words and Music by
David J. Matthews and Glen Ballard

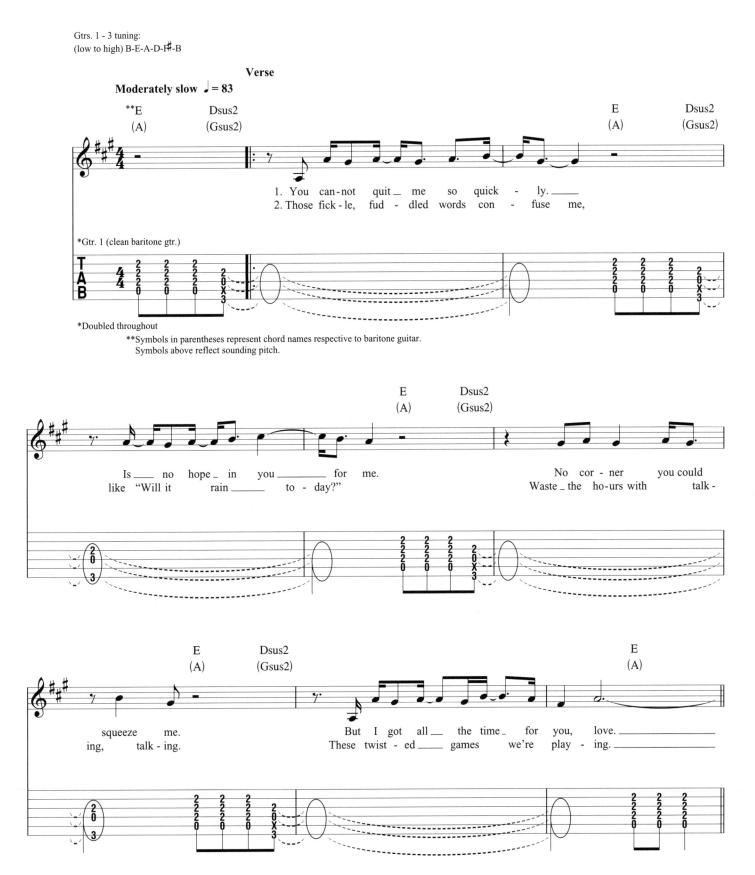

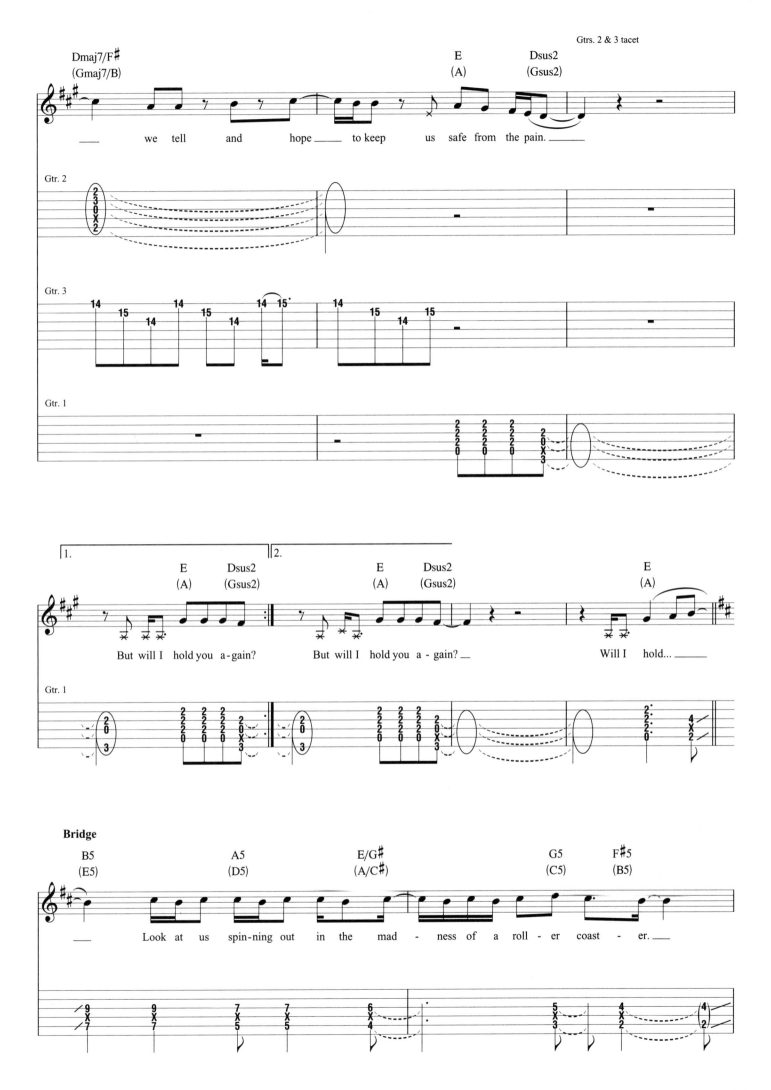

GETTING YOUR TWANG ON

Now that you've gotten your feet wet with some open chords, let's start getting down with some twang. Players like Duane Eddy (the "King of Twang") made this style their bread and butter in the late '50s/early '60s, but twang has also been a fairly regular occurrence in country music throughout the years. Players such as session ace Brent Mason and Pete Anderson (Dwight Yoakam's right-hand man), among others, regularly make use of them in their arsenal, on a myriad of tracks.

TONE TIPS

For the twang sound, you'll want to use a fairly clean-toned amp, such as a Fender Twin, and boost the treble a generous amount. If you have more than one pickup on your guitar, use the bridge pickup for maximum twang (the other pickup settings are certainly useful, as well), and pick near the bridge to brighten the sound even more.

A tremolo pedal is often a nice touch, as well. Set the depth control fairly high and adjust the rate for the song (most songs use a fairly quick rate). For country styles, in particular, a compressor pedal will help provide a consistent attack. Set it for a moderate amount of compression—no need to squash it to death—so that you can still hear a clear pick attack.

OPEN MAJOR PENTATONIC SCALES

Three open major pentatonic scales see quite a bit of action on the baritone: B (E) major pentatonic, D (G) major pentatonic, and E (A) major pentatonic. In case you aren't already familiar with these, let's look at them now.

B (E) Major Pentatonic Scale

TRACK 11

D (G) Major Pentatonic Scale

TRACK 12

E (A) Major Pentatonic Scale

TRACK 13

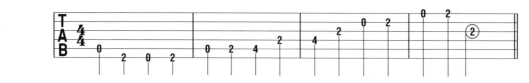

OPEN MINOR PENTATONIC SCALES

Let's also look at two open minor pentatonic scales: E (A) minor pentatonic and B (E) minor pentatonic.

E (A) Minor Pentatonic Scale

TRACK 14

B (E) Minor Pentatonic Scale

Notice that this is the relative minor of the previously shown D (G) major pentatonic. Therefore, they share the same notes; the only difference lies in which note is considered the tonic.

TRACK 15

PENTATONIC TWANG RIFFS

Now let's check out some riffs from these scales. As you'll see, it's common to employ slides, hammer-ons, pull-offs, and bends in these types of riffs.

E (A) Major Pentatonic

TRACK 16

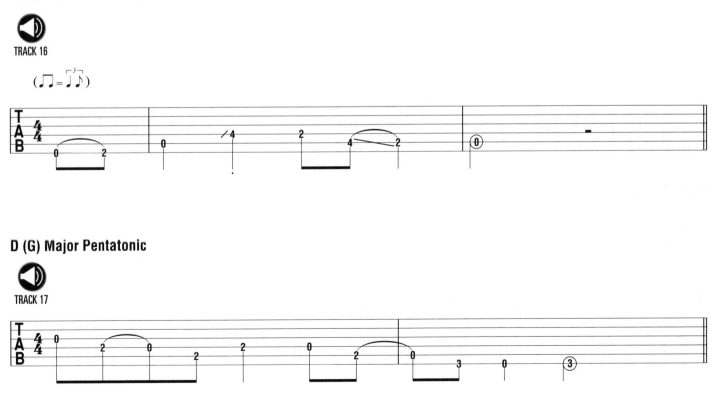

D (G) Major Pentatonic

TRACK 17

B (E) Major Pentatonic

TRACK 18

B (E) Major Pentatonic

TRACK 19

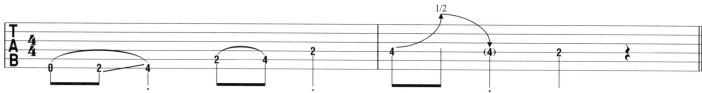

E (A) Minor Pentatonic

TRACK 20

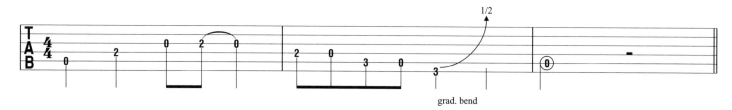

grad. bend

B (E) Minor Pentatonic

TRACK 21

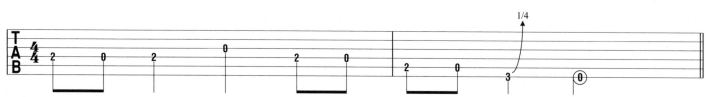

"A LITTLE PAST LITTLE ROCK"

Now let's check out some songs and hear some of these riffs in action. First up is "A Little Past Little Rock" by Lee Ann Womack. Brent Mason dresses up the intro to this song with a twangy baritone line that's mostly derived from the open E (A) major pentatonic scale. For this song, Brent has his sixth string tuned down a whole step to A. You can think of this as akin to drop D tuning on a standard guitar. Just tune your sixth string down a whole step so that it sounds one octave lower than your open fourth string.

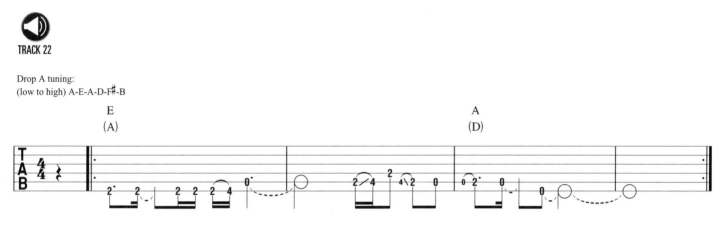

"LITTLE WAYS"

Next up is Dwight Yoakam's "Little Ways." Aside from peppering the song with baritone fills throughout, Pete Anderson takes a twangy solo that would make Duane proud. Pete worked out of two scales here: A (D) major pentatonic over the A (D) chord, and E (A) major pentatonic over the E (A) chord. Here's a fingering for the A (D) major pentatonic, which we haven't looked at yet:

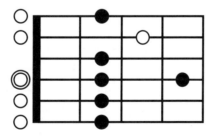

However, just as in "A Little Past Little Rock," Pete is tuned to drop A tuning here, so he's afforded one extra low note on the bottom of the A (D) major pentatonic form, which happens to be the tonic. And he certainly makes it count!

Drop A tuning:
(low to high) A-E-A-D-F#-B

"GALVESTON"

Country crooner and guitar virtuoso Glen Campbell employed the baritone in several of his hits, as well. The 1969 hit "Galveston" is a fine example. Glen used a moveable major pentatonic form, based off the open E (A) major pentatonic form, for most of this riff. He played in F (Bb) here, so the form looks like this:

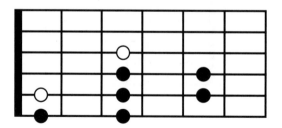

Be sure to compare this form to the open E (A) form to see how it was derived. Now kick on some tremolo and play along with this classic. (**Note:** The original recording sounds about a quarter step sharp.)

"BONNIE CAME BACK"

And now let's rock out with the "King of Twang" himself. "Bonnie Came Back" is basically Duane Eddy's arrangement of the traditional Scottish folk song "My Bonnie Lies Over the Ocean." His twang is in prime form here, and he makes use of several different ranges on his baritone, playing the melody in two different octaves.

Although most of the melody comes from the A (D) major pentatonic scale, there are a few notes from the seven-note major scale. Here's the A (D) major scale in open position:

A (D) Major Scale

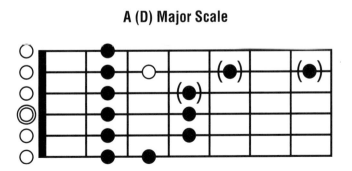

BONNIE CAME BACK

Words and Music by
Duane Eddy and Lee Hazlewood

TRACK 25

*Symbols in parentheses represent chord names respective to baritone guitar.
Symbols above reflect sounding pitch.

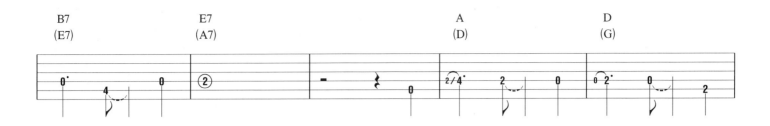

D.S. al Coda

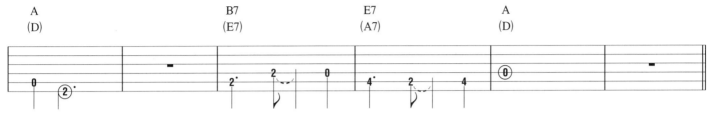

⊕ Coda

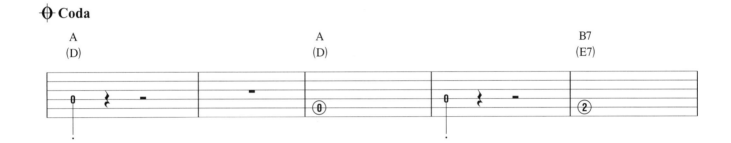

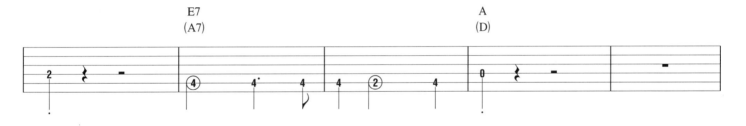

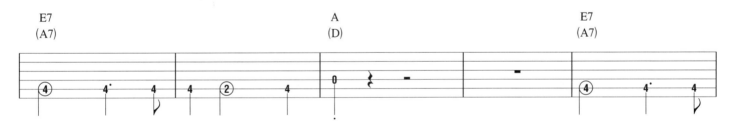

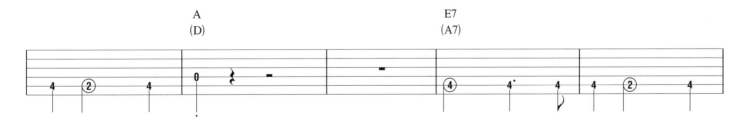

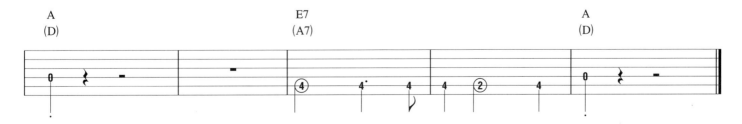

USING THE BARITONE AS A TEXTURE

The baritone is obviously capable of making a big, bold statement, but it's also an awesome tool for adding texture to a song. This makes it an indispensable item to have around if you have a home studio, for example. In this chapter, we'll explore several options in this regard that will make the idea of seeing the baritone as a niche instrument seem downright silly.

TIC-TAC BASS

The first texture we'll look at is the "tic-tac bass" sound that was heard so often in the Nashville recordings of the '60s and '70s. The idea is that a palm-muted baritone guitar would play along with the upright bass—often doubling it but sometimes adding its own lines—to provide definition. It was commonly played through a clean Fender amp (such as a Deluxe), often with a bit of reverb added for a "splash" of sound after the attack. Set the amp tone quite bright for this style. The bass is providing the bottom; the baritone is providing the attack.

Let's check out some examples. Below is a country-style shuffle idea in C (F). Notice that we're doubling a lot of what the bass is doing, but we're also adding a few connecting notes from the C (F) major pentatonic scale.

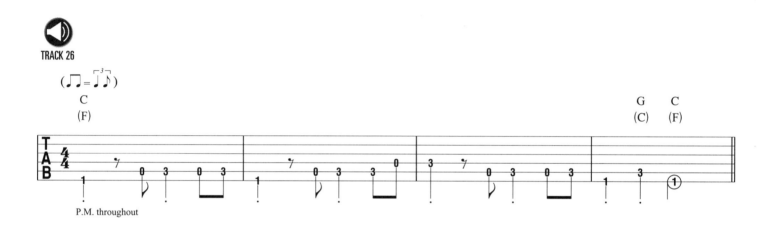

And here's an example that has a bit of a spaghetti western sound to it. Again, we're hitting mostly root notes while adding a few connecting tones in between.

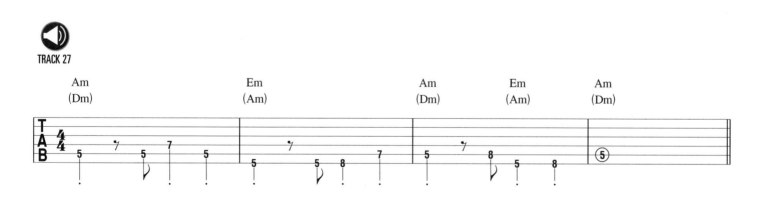

"CRAZY"

Now let's check out how the pros do it. "Crazy," penned by a 27-year-old Willie Nelson, was a smash hit for Patsy Cline in 1961 and has remained one of the most enduring country standards of all to this day. It features a classic example of the tic-tac bass style throughout the track. We'll play it here in Patsy's key, Bb (Eb) major. (**Note:** In the original recording, the song modulates up a half step for the final verse, but we won't include that section here.)

Throughout the song, the baritone plays a combination of mostly arpeggio tones and connecting tones—often chromatic— to navigate the song's many changes. It's unclear as to whether the baritone was tuned E to E (an octave lower than a standard guitar) or B to B in the original song, but here it's been arranged for our B-to-B tuning. Generally speaking, you try to go low with this type of thing when you can, but if you can't, it's OK. The palm mute and heavy string gauges are the most important aspects of the sound.

CRAZY

Words and Music by Willie Nelson

TRACK 28

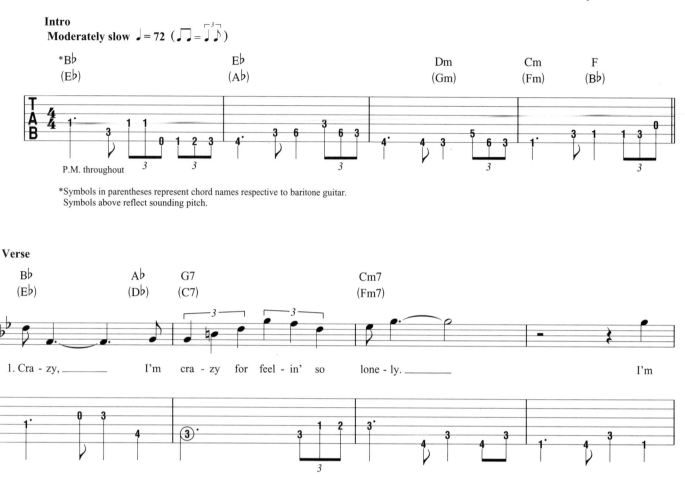

*Symbols in parentheses represent chord names respective to baritone guitar.
Symbols above reflect sounding pitch.

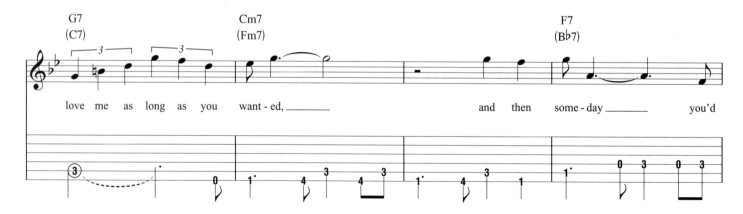

DOUBLING OR HARMONIZING A STANDARD GUITAR

The baritone can also be just the thing you need to add some girth or chime to a standard guitar part. This can be doubling at the same pitch, at an octave below, or at another interval, such as a 5th. Regardless, the unique tone of the baritone always adds a distinctive touch. Let's hear some examples of this.

First up, we have this D minor pentatonic riff played on a standard guitar:

TRACK 29

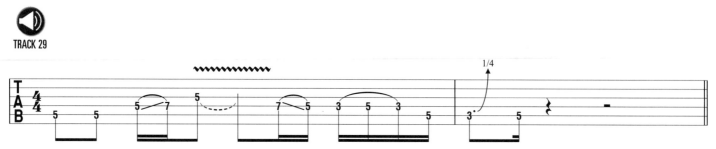

Now let's see what we can do with it. In order to double it at the same pitch on the baritone, we need to play the same thing a 4th higher. In other words, we need to move everything to the next higher string set. Remember: if the second string is involved, you'll need to compensate for that in your fingering. So, below is the same riff, doubled at the same pitch on the baritone. This will provide a basic thickening of the tone. It's similar to the effect you get when you double a standard guitar riff, but it's a little thicker-sounding with the baritone.

TRACK 30

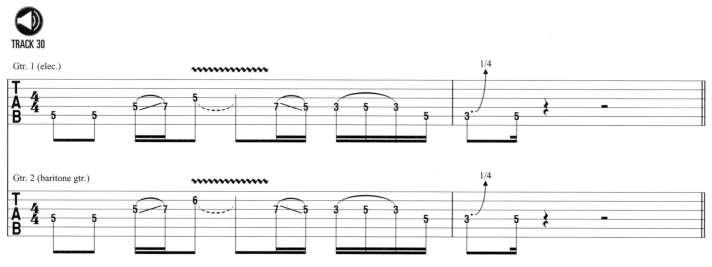

So, the rule for doubling a standard guitar at the same pitch on the baritone (tuned B to B) is the following:

- Move everything to the next higher (thinner) string set (and remember to account for string 2 if it's used).

Now let's double this riff an octave lower with the baritone. To do this, we'll need to move down one string set and back two frets. This will really add some girth to the original guitar track!

TRACK 31

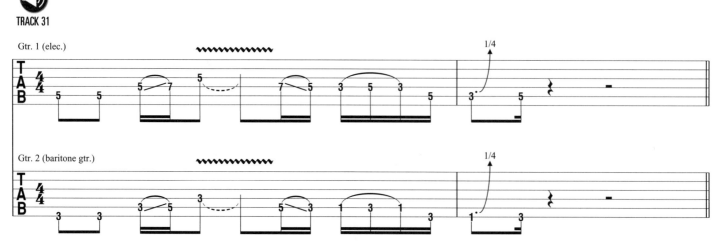

So, the rule for doubling a standard guitar an octave lower on the baritone (tuned B to B) is the following:

- Move everything to the next lower (thicker) string set and back two frets (and remember to account for string 2 if it's used).

And what happens if we just play the same exact thing on the baritone that we play on a standard guitar? Well, we harmonize the standard guitar a 4th lower, which sounds *really* thick and can be quite an awesome effect in some instances.

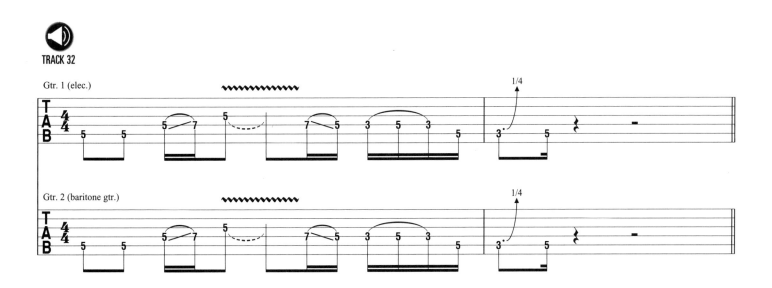

This can sound really cool on all kinds of things—not just muscular low-register riffs. For example, below is a clean-tone arpeggio riff in D minor on standard guitar. When we play the same exact thing on baritone, it sounds awesome.

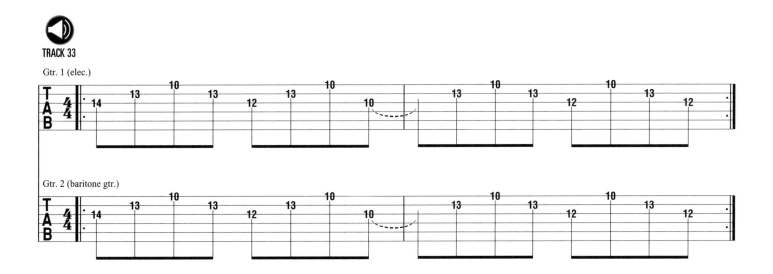

So, you should definitely experiment with this idea. Oftentimes, it will sound very interesting, if not outright amazing. In the event that you run into one or two notes that don't work, it's usually not difficult to quickly adjust those notes for the baritone track.

THE BARITONE'S CHARM

Sometimes, it's not about the twang. Sometimes, the baritone just sounds absolutely lovely playing a melody in that low register. Add a bit of tremolo—or maybe some delay—and try playing a stately melody on those low strings. It can really bring a song to life sometimes.

Here's an idea in D (G) based on the D (G) major scale. We're just adding a bit of delay and letting the baritone do its thing.

TRACK 34

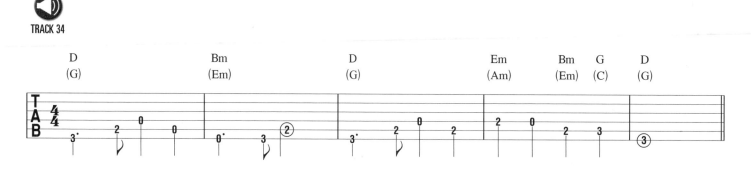

This next one is in B (E) and adds a bit of tremolo—a match made in heaven.

TRACK 35

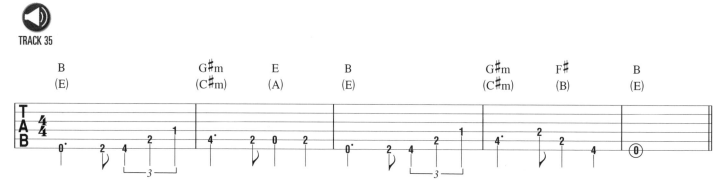

"TWIN PEAKS THEME"

The theme to David Lynch's short-lived TV show *Twin Peaks* is a prime example of baritone magic. Largely based off F (B♭) major pentatonic, the simple intro melody is performed hauntingly on a clean-toned baritone treated to tremolo.

TRACK 36

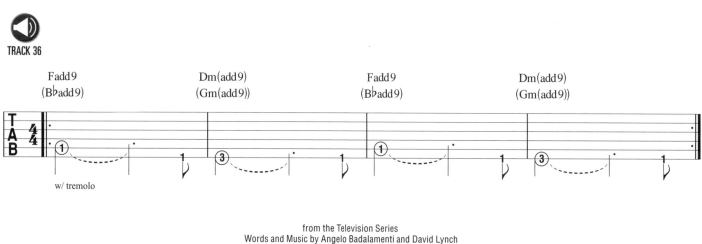

from the Television Series
Words and Music by Angelo Badalamenti and David Lynch
Copyright © 1990 ANLON MUSIC and O.K. PAUL MUSIC
All Rights Controlled and Administered by UNIVERSAL MUSIC CORP. and SONGS OF UNIVERSAL, INC.
All Rights Reserved   Used by Permission

ROCK AND METAL

Ever since drop tuning became popular in the rock and metal genres in the '90s, the baritone has naturally begun to show up more and more to join the riffery fun. The baritone is pre-fabricated to churn out those low, aggressive riffs and therefore is a perfect addition to any metal player's arsenal.

SINGLE-NOTE RIFFS

This is not to say that the baritone had no place before this new breed of hard rock/metal. It would occasionally make an appearance in the riffs of the '70s and '80s, as well. Many of these riffs made use of minor scales, such as the natural minor or Dorian. Here are some common moveable scale forms for those two scales:

Natural Minor Scale

Form 1

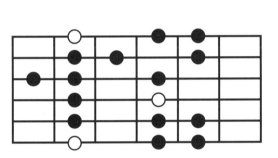

Form 2

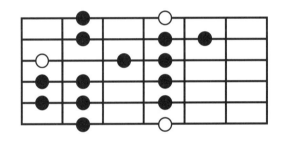

Dorian Mode

Form 1

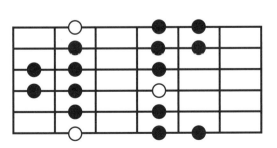

Form 2

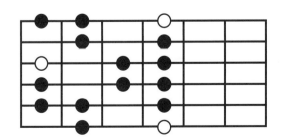

The baritone's girth lends an unmistakable quality to single-note riffs. Let's check out a few examples. This first is in E (A) Dorian and uses Form 2, which puts us in second position. Note that the open low B (E) string is included, as well.

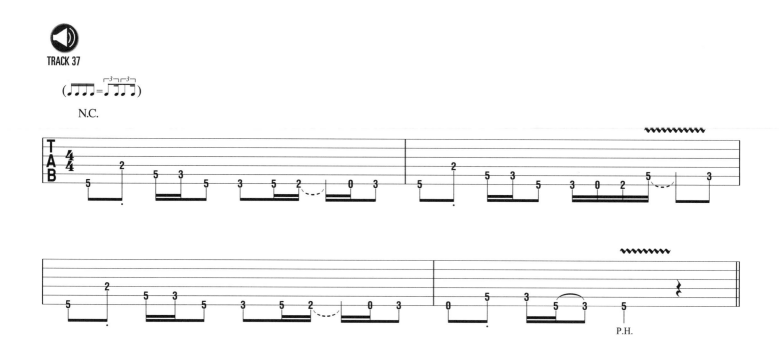

And here's one from the C♯ (F♯) minor pentatonic scale in second position, along with the open B (E) string. This is the same as the open B (E) minor pentatonic scale we looked at back on page 28, only two frets higher.

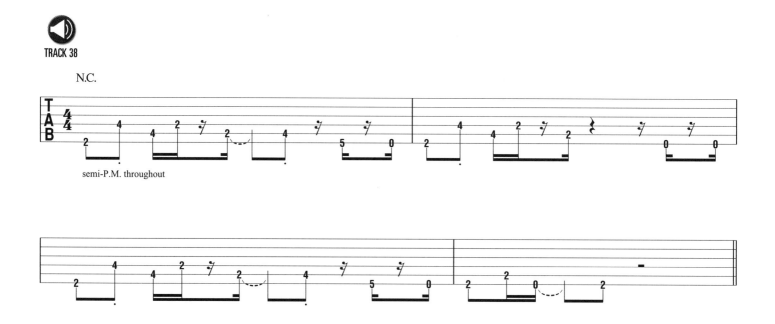

"ROCK LOBSTER"

The B-52's Ricky Wilson had a very unorthodox style for sure. He usually played a Mosrite guitar with the middle two strings removed, and his tunings were all over the place. According to interviews, he would simply "twist the tuning pegs until something sounded good." One of the signature songs from their first album, "Rock Lobster" was not performed on a baritone guitar, but it sure sounds that way. Ricky had his two lowest strings tuned a major 3rd (the equivalent of four frets) lower than normal when he pounded out the song's minor-scale hook. Playing in an open E minor position, this meant the song sounded in C minor.

Since we have our baritones tuned B to B, we'll play it a half step lower, in B minor. (If you want to play along with the original, you could always place a capo on fret 1, and you'd be good to go.) Ricky's using Form 1 of the natural minor scale in open position.

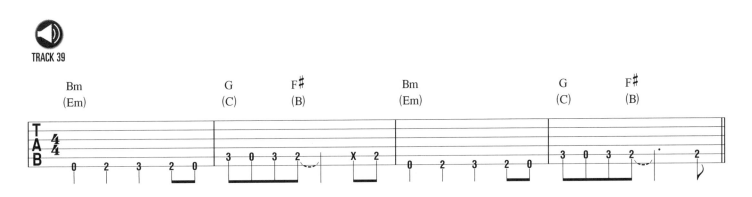

"BACK IN THE SADDLE"

No stranger to muscular guitar riffs, Aerosmith's Joe Perry enlisted the services of the famous Fender Bass VI for "Back in the Saddle," from the 1977 release *Rocks*. As discussed earlier, whether or not the Bass VI, which is tuned a full octave lower than a standard guitar, qualifies as a baritone guitar is up for debate. Regardless, we can still play a great-sounding arrangement of the riff on a B-to-B-tuned bari; we just won't be able to play it quite as low as the original recording. Joe's playing out of E minor on the original recording, but Aerosmith tuned down a half step for this song, so his Fender Bass VI was actually tuned E♭ to E♭.

Joe works from the Dorian mode here, primarily making use of the second of the two scale forms previously shown, only moved over one string set so that the tonic is on string 5 instead of string 6 (he also adds in a few chromatic passing tones). It looks like this:

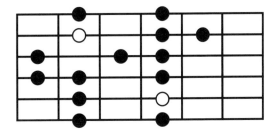

We'll play the song in G minor (C minor), which is the lowest we can get on a B-to-B bari while still using the same fingering pattern that Joe uses. Kick on some distortion (although not *too* much—listen to the original recording) and get down and dirty!

TRACK 40

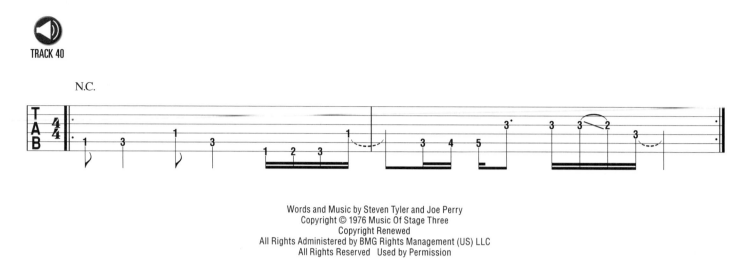

"INVISIBLE KID"

For this song, off Metallica's *St. Anger* album (2003), James Hetfield uses his signature ESP Viper baritone to lay down a furious riff that kicks off the song with a kick in the teeth. He's tuned to drop A (D), down a half step for this song. In other words, from low to high: Ab–Eb–Ab–Db–F–Bb. However, we'll play it here in drop A (D) tuning, so it will sound a half step higher than the original recording.

James is using only two notes here, in two different octaves, to create this riff, proving that many times attitude is the most important thing in a great riff.

TRACK 41

Drop A tuning:
(low to high) A-E-A-D-F#-B

Intro
Moderately fast Rock ♩ = 164

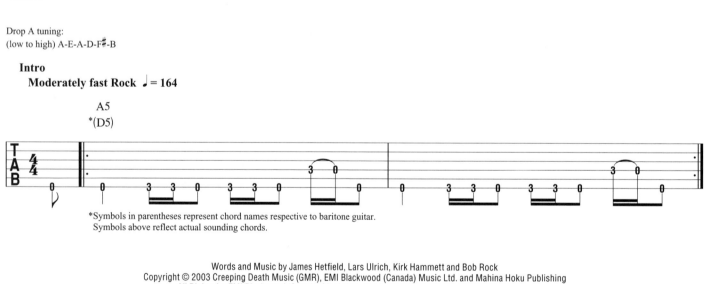

*Symbols in parentheses represent chord names respective to baritone guitar.
Symbols above reflect actual sounding chords.

POWER CHORD RIFFS

Of course, rock and metal wouldn't be the same without the mighty power chord, and the baritone certainly has plenty to say on the subject. We'll look at two possibilities in this regard: standard baritone tuning and drop tuning.

Standard Baritone Tuning Power Chords

This is the same power chord form as on a standard guitar. They're usually played in two- or three-string versions, as follows:

Sixth-String Root

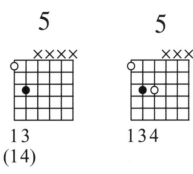

Fifth-String Root

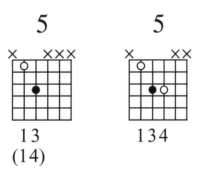

Needless to say, these forms sound innately heavy on the baritone. Here are a few examples of that:

TRACK 42

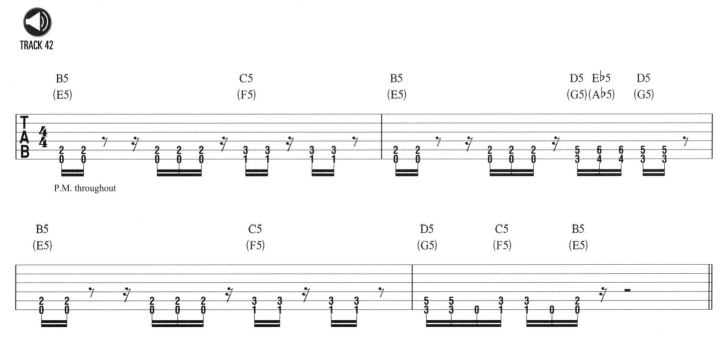

TRACK 43

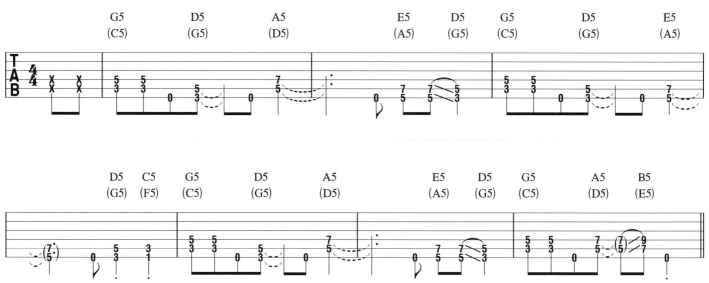

"LIE"

John Petrucci's ultra-heavy riff from Dream Theater's "Lie," though performed on a seven-string Music Man guitar with a low B string, sits perfectly on a baritone guitar, as his lower strings are tuned exactly the same.

TRACK 44

Intro
Moderate rock ♩ = 94

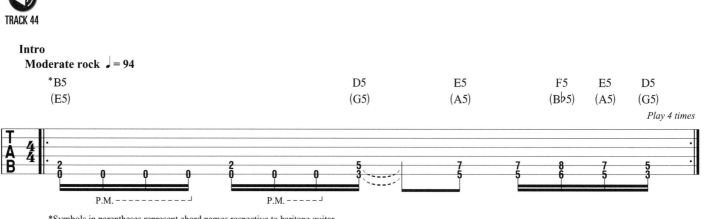

*Symbols in parentheses represent chord names respective to baritone guitar.
Symbols above reflect sounding pitch.

Drop Tuning Power Chords

By "drop tuning," we mean that the sixth string is dropped down a whole step to A so that it's one octave lower than your fourth string. This means, of course, that you have one-finger power chords in the sixth-string root form!

Sixth-String Root

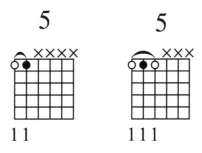

As a result, active riffs are made much easier:

TRACK 45

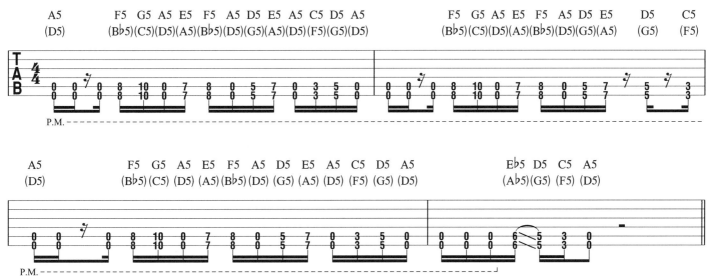

"MY OWN SUMMER (SHOVE IT)"

Stephen Carpenter has made a habit of fueling Deftones songs with detuned riffage, and this song is no exception. The original recording sounds in the key of D♭, as he's in a drop D tuning, down a half step. But we'll play it here in drop A (D) tuning, which will sound two whole steps lower.

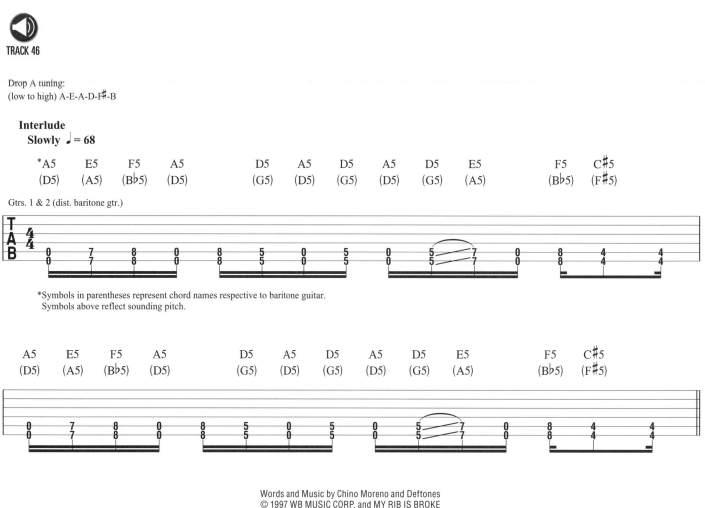

TRACK 46

Drop A tuning:
(low to high) A-E-A-D-F♯-B

Interlude
Slowly ♩ = 68

Gtrs. 1 & 2 (dist. baritone gtr.)

*Symbols in parentheses represent chord names respective to baritone guitar.
Symbols above reflect sounding pitch.

Drop Tuning Sus2 Chords

If you play the three-string power-chord form and add your ring or pinky finger two frets higher on string 4, you get a great-sounding sus2 chord.

Sixth-String Root

sus2

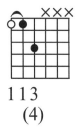

When combined with power chords, you can get some very colorful riffs.

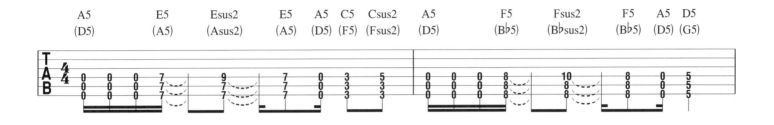

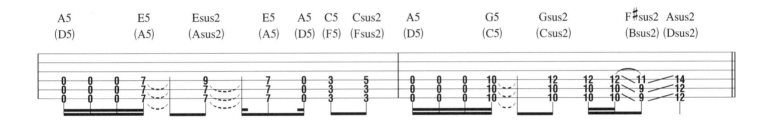

ADDITIONAL THINGS TO KEEP IN MIND

Aside from everything we've covered thus far, there are a few other factors to consider when playing the baritone guitar. In this final section, we'll take a look at some additional useful tips that may come in handy in a variety of situations.

THICKER STRINGS, TOUGHER BENDS

Before you launch into several of your pet licks at the local open jam session, keep in mind that bending on a baritone guitar feels a bit different than on a standard guitar. This is particularly noticeable with the third string, which will be wound on a typical set of baritone electric strings. This means that a whole-step bend on that string requires significantly more effort than on a standard guitar. It's not impossible by any means, but it's certainly not a walk in the park either, especially down on the lower frets.

Downward bends (pulling down toward the floor) on the lower-pitched strings require more strength, too. It's a good idea to practice these bends with the following exercises to make sure you're getting all the way there.

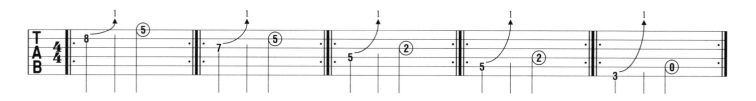

HOW FAR IS THAT STRETCH, AGAIN?

By the same token, a longer scale length means larger-spaced frets. This may mean that some of those three-notes-per-string scale patterns or cluster voicings may be out of reach on the lower frets. So, before you whip out that Paul Gilbert lick on your first gig with the bari, you may want to do a reality check first on the longer scale length and possibly adjust some fingerings.

For example, if the last part of this C Mixolydian lick is too uncomfortable:

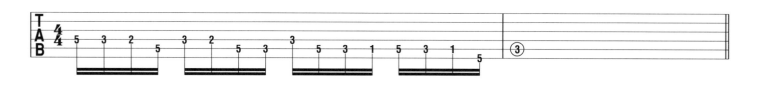

You may need to move some of the notes down a string to keep the stretches manageable, as demonstrated here:

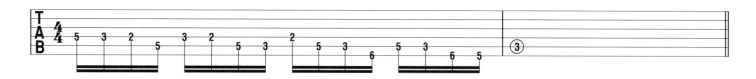

TOO MUDDY FOR COMFORT?

As mentioned when we looked at open chords, certain voicings tend to sound a bit too muddy on the bari, depending on the tone and context. The good news is that there are alternatives. For example, instead of playing these D (G) voicings:

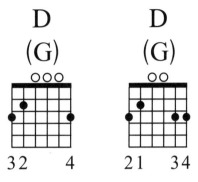

You can simply mute string 5 to clear up the muddiness:

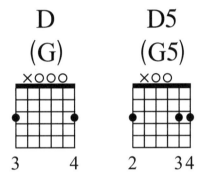

Or, if this G (C) chord sounds a bit muddy because of the low 3rd interval:

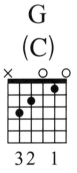

You can simply mute string 4:

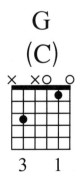

Or you could get around both problems by using barre chords instead:

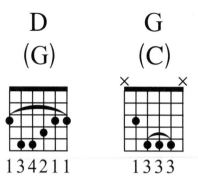

JAMMING WITH OTHERS (WHO AREN'T PLAYING A BARI)

While we've demonstrated throughout this book that baritones have many uses, the fact remains that they aren't the most popular instrument on the block. Chances are, if you're jamming with a band, there won't be two baritone guitars.

This means you're likely to be the "odd man out," and you'll essentially be playing the song in a different key than the rest of the band. In other words, if you look to the other guitar player or bass player for visual cues on the chords, you're in for a rude awakening.

So, let's look at a few tips and shortcuts that will help you navigate these sometimes-tricky waters.

Doubling a Riff

If you simply want to double a riff that's played by the guitar or bass player, you can use the rules we discussed back on page 38. To summarize once more:

- **To double a standard guitar at the same pitch on the baritone (tuned B to B):** Move everything to the next higher (thinner) string set (and remember to account for string 2 if it's used).

- **To double a standard guitar an octave lower on the baritone (tuned B to B):** Move everything to the next lower (thicker) string set and back two frets (and remember to account for string 2 if it's used).

So, to double this standard guitar riff:

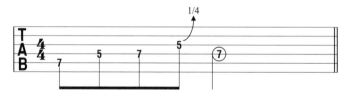

You would play this:

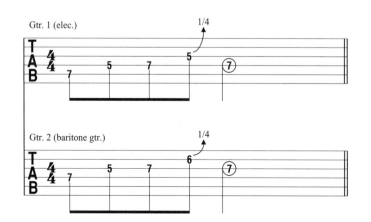

To play an octave lower on the baritone, you would play this:

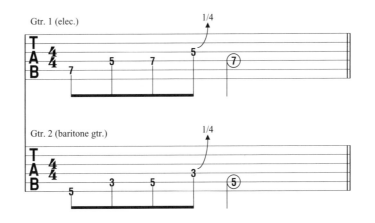

Playing a Chord Progression

In order to play chords from a chart, you'll need to think it through a bit more. The best way, in my opinion, is to use the number (or Roman numeral) system. This is the way all those Nashville session players are able to crank out professional backing tracks in no time at all, even if they're asked to change keys before a new take.

The basic idea is that you assign a number to each chord in a key in the same way you assign numbers to scale degrees. So, in the key of C, for example, you have the C major scale:

C	D	E	F	G	A	B
1	2	3	4	5	6	7

If you played chords (triads) for each of those notes, you'd have the harmonized C major scale. When you add Roman numerals or numbers to those chords, you can see how the system works:

	C	Dm	Em	F	G	Am	B°
Roman numerals:	I	ii	iii	IV	V	vi	vii°
Nashville numbers:	1	2–	3–	4	5	6–	7°

As you can see, the Roman numeral system uses uppercase for major chords and lowercase for minor chords. The Nashville system simply uses numbers, adding a dash (or hyphen) for minor chords. Both systems add a "°" for a diminished chord.

So, how is this helpful? Well, every major key uses the same formula of major and minor chords. In other words, it's always **major–minor–minor–major–major–minor–diminished**. Therefore, once you know your key signatures, you can apply this shorthand system to any progression.

For example, let's say you have a song in C, with a chord progression of C–G–Am–F, and you want to play along on your bari. Well, the first thing you'd do is convert that progression to numbers (or numerals). To do this, just write out the major scale and then write the chord formula beneath it, adding the appropriate chord suffixes as you go.

C	Dm	Em	F	G	Am	B°
I	ii	iii	**IV**	**V**	**vi**	vii°

So, a C–G–Am–F progression in C is represented as I–V–vi–IV.

Now, to play the song on the baritone guitar, you're going to use the IV chord as your new I chord. In other words, you'll play in the key of F, since F is the IV chord in C:

C	D	E	F
1	2	3	**4**

Now, write out the F major scale and add the appropriate chord suffixes.

F	Gm	Am	B♭	C	Dm	E°
I	ii	iii	IV	V	vi	vii°

Now match the Roman numeral progression to the appropriate chords in F:

F	Gm	Am	**B♭**	**C**	**Dm**	E°
I	ii	iii	**IV**	**V**	**vi**	vii°

Therefore, the progression on the baritone guitar will be **F–C–Dm–B♭**.

Let's do another one quickly. Let's say we have this progression in the key of D: D–Bm–Em–A. By writing out our chords in D major, we see that this is a I–vi–ii–V progression:

D	**Em**	F#m	G	**A**	**Bm**	C#°
I	**ii**	iii	IV	**V**	**vi**	vii°

Now take the IV chord (G) and make that your new I chord. Then write out the chords in that key (G):

G	**Am**	Bm	C	**D**	**Em**	F#°
I	**ii**	iii	IV	**V**	**vi**	vii°

And there you have it: Your progression on the bari is **G–Em–Am–D**.

The good news is that you can use this to play in any key. The bad news is that you need to learn your key signatures in order to do it. But that's a small price to pay for such freedom. Once you begin to learn key signatures, you'll realize that there's nothing to it, as it's a very formulaic process.

But what about minor progressions? Well, we use the same process; we just use different numbers. The key of A minor, for example, would look like this:

Am	B°	C	Dm	Em	F	G
i	ii°	♭III	iv	v	♭VI	♭VII

Therefore, the key of D minor would look like this:

Dm	E°	F	Gm	Am	B♭	C
i	ii°	♭III	iv	v	♭VI	♭VII

And so on.

Again, you need to know your major and minor scales to make this work. You can even handle non-diatonic chords (ones that are outside the key) with this method. Let's say you have this progression in C major: C–E–F–A♭. Well, by looking at our harmonized C major scale, we can see that the E and the A♭ chords are non-diatonic. But we can reflect this with our Roman numeral system. It would simply look like this:

C	E	F	A♭
I	III	IV	♭VI

- The C and F are the same.

- The E chord is still built on the 3rd degree of the scale (E), but it's changed to major, so we use an uppercase numeral.

- The A♭ is built on the ♭6th degree (A♭) instead of the 6th (A), so we add a "♭" symbol on the Roman numeral and make it uppercase to indicate a major chord.

To transpose this progression for the bari, we'd play it in F (the IV chord of C). And it would look like this:

F	A	B♭	D♭
I	III	IV	♭VI

If you master this method, you'll be able to apply it in many different ways. For example, you can use the same technique when playing with a capo (it's the same principle) or when a singer needs you to transpose a song to better fit his/her vocal range. By converting a progression to numerals, you only need to remember those numerals. Then you can overlay it onto any key you wish—once you learn your key signatures, of course!

RHYTHM TAB LEGEND

Rhythm Tab is a form of notation that adds rhythmic values to the traditional tab staff.

TABLATURE graphically represents the guitar fingerboard. Each horizontal line represents a string, and each number represents a fret. Rhythmic values are shown using ovals, stems, and dots.

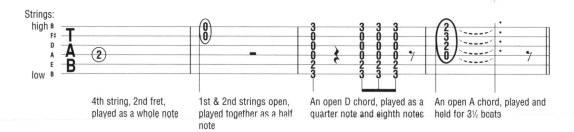

4th string, 2nd fret, played as a whole note

1st & 2nd strings open, played together as a half note

An open D chord, played as a quarter note and eighth notes

An open A chord, played and hold for 3½ beats

Definitions for Special Guitar Notation

HALF-STEP BEND: Strike the note and bend up 1/2 step.

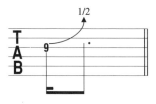

WHOLE-STEP BEND: Strike the note and bend up one step.

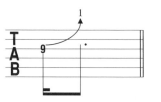

SLIGHT (MICROTONE) BEND: Strike the note and bend up 1/4 step.

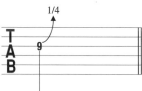

BEND AND RELEASE: Strike the note and bend up as indicated, then release back to the original note. Only the first note is struck.

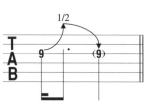

PRE-BEND: Bend the note as indicated, then strike it.

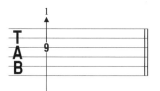

GRACE NOTE PRE-BEND AND RELEASE: Bend the note as indicated. Strike it and release the bend back to the original note.

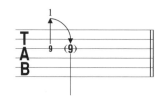

UNISON BEND: Strike the two notes simultaneously and bend the lower note up to the pitch of the higher.

HOLD BEND: While sustaining bent note, strike note on different string.

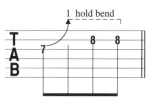

VIBRATO: The string is vibrated by rapidly bending and releasing the note with the fretting hand.

WIDE VIBRATO: The pitch is varied to a greater degree by vibrating with the fretting hand.

HAMMER-ON: Strike the first (lower) note with one finger, then sound the higher note (on the same string) with another finger by fretting it without picking.

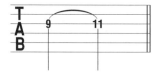

PULL-OFF: Place both fingers on the notes to be sounded. Strike the first note and without picking, pull the finger off to sound the second (lower) note.

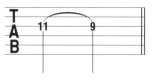

HAMMER FROM NOWHERE: Sound note(s) by hammering with fret hand finger only.

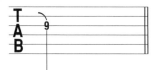

GRACE NOTE SLUR: Strike the note and immediately hammer-on (or pull-off) as indicated.

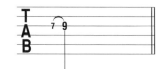

GRACE NOTE SLUR (CLUSTER): Strike the notes and immediately hammer-on (or pull-off) as indicated.

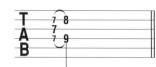

LEGATO SLIDE: Strike the first note and then slide the same fret-hand finger up or down to the second note. The second note is not struck.

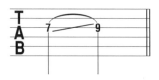